I0617325

Environmental Lifestyle Guide

For Grade 10 Students

VOL.3 OF 11

Fasion & Textile

Jahangir Asadi

Vancouver, BC CANADA

Copyright © 2022 by **SILOSA** Consulting Group Inc.

All rights reserved. No part of this publication may be reproduced, distributed or transmitted in any form or by any means, including photocopying, recording, or other electronic or mechanical methods, without the prior written permission of the publisher, except in the case of brief quotations embodied in critical reviews and certain other noncommercial uses permitted by copyright law. For permission requests, write to the publisher, addressed "Attention: Permissions Coordinator," at the address below.

Published by: Silosa Consulting Group Inc.
Vancouver, BC **CANADA**
Email: Info@Silosa.ca
www.silosa.ca

Ordering Information:
Quantity sales. Special discounts are available on quantity purchases by universities, schools, corporations, associations, and others. For details, contact the "Sales Department" at the above mentioned email address.

Environmental lifestyle Guide Vol.3 for Grade.10/J.Asadi —1st ed.
ISBN: 978-1-990451-77-5

Contents

We hope that, 10,000 years from now, future generations will be able to see flowers that provide bees with nectar and pollen and...
BEES provide flowers with the means to reproduce by spreading pollen from flower to flower,....

Jahangir Asadi

This book is dedicated to my professor, Dr.Sadeq Fakhr

Every possible effort has been made to ensure that the information contained in this book is accurate at the time of going to press, and the publishers and the author cannot accept responsibility for any errors or omissions, however caused. No responsibility for loss or damage occasioned to any person acting, or refraining from action, as a result of the material in this publication can be accepted by the publisher or the author.

Introduction

This book is part of an eleven volume series that is meant to be a standard textbook series, for grades 9 to 12. TTAIN & ESFK & SCG improves quality of life and reduces environmental degradation by fostering new consumption patterns and sustainable lifestyles through International Cooperative Extension Service programs at houses, offices, schools and libraries all over the globe.

Climate change is real. Therefore people have the potential to make a difference now and for future generations. This book provides climate science basics, including the roles that lifestyles and populations play in the climate scenario, the significance of carbon footprints, and an overview of the current climate situation. The manual has been categorized based on humanity's needs starting first with food and ending with tourism. The manual then illustrates the difference between adaptation (taking steps to live with the changes) and mitigation (taking steps to slow the rate of change.)

Adaptation examples include food, energy, transportation, recreation. Mitigation focuses on effectively engaging with local governments, through serving on advisory boards, communicating with public officials, educational institutes, schools, universities, libraries and leading communities towards climate change actions.

One useful way to mitigate climate change is through increasing public knowledge to better understand the impact of the rate of change on plants and animals. This is crucial for preserving species; and for assessing potential insects and disease outbreaks in agriculture, natural resources and public health.

Taking personal action is a key element of this manual.

Citizens are challenged to consume 20% fewer resources, to bring world consumption levels down as much as possible. Readers are given 12 practical steps to take to make the changes. The resources section provides additional information, and readers are encouraged to contact the author for further questions.

As an accessibility action, we have provided Online international courses on climate change control as well. You can access the courses via the following link:

http://TopTenAward.org

SILOSA Consulting Group (SCG)

Silosa Consulting Group (SCG) was established to provide outstanding consulting services of management system & educational standards to individuals, groups, companies, schools, and organizations all over the globe. SCG is publishing an "Environmental Lifestyle Guide " book series as a standard textbook related to increasing environmental awareness of students means being aware of the natural environment and making choices that benefit the earth, rather than hurt it. Vol.1 to 11 (for grades 9 to 12) providing some of the ways to practice environmental awareness include: **Recycling**, **Conserving energy and water**, **Reuse, Activism, and others**.

SCG book publishing services and distribution services are connected to over 39,000 booksellers worldwide, including Apple, Amazon, Barnes & Noble, Indigo, Google Play Books, and many more. SCG has enough experiences to help create new and effective environmental educational programmes in different countries all over the world. For more detail, visit our website : http://silosa.ca and/or send your enquirer to the following email:

info@silosa.ca

CHAPTER 1

About ISO 14000 for Students

The International Organization for Standardization is an independent, non-governmental organization, the members of which are the standards organizations of the 165 member countries. It is the world's largest developer of voluntary international standards and it facilitates world trade by providing common standards among nations. More than twenty thousand standards have been set, covering everything from manufactured products and technology to food safety, agriculture, and healthcare.

Kids ISO 14000s
"Kids ISO 14000s" is a new environmental education program for children, based on ISO 14000s, which is international standard for environmental management. Primary aims of this program are: -
1. To teach and train children how to manage the environmental issues (such as energy saving) by themselves through the working book and guide book of this program,
2. To certify those children who showed good accomplishment in the program from highly international authority (as is the case of ISO 14000s)
3. To network those children through the international network (Kids International Network), so that the children can work on the environment, internationally.

2. System of Kids ISO 14000s Program
The system of Kids ISO 14000s Program consists of
1. Operation Headquarter (ArTech).
2. Workbook, Guidebook (originally published by ArTech, and local versions are produced by each countries).
3. Eco-Kids-Instructors for local operation and evaluation of the performance of the children.
4. International accreditation committee for accreditation of accomplishment of the children, for certification of the Eco-Kids-Instructors, as well as overall checks of this program.
5. Linkage with international organizations (such as UNU, UNESCO, etc. …) And also national organizations

More information can be obtained :

www.ISO.org

Canada

Environmental Sustain for Future kids established in Vancouver, BC Canada in 2020. (ESFK) is an international ecolabel focused on taking care of environment for future of kids. ESFK defined as 'self-declared' environmental claims made by manufacturers and businesses based on ISO 14020 series of standards, the claimant can declare the environmental objectives and targets in relation to taking care of environment for future kids.
However, this declaration will be verifiable.

Environmental Sustain for Future Kids
Vancouver, BC CANADA

Email: info@esfk.org
Web: www.esfk.org

STEP THREE

Fashion and textile

The textile industry being a very good example for the most advancing and ecologically harmful industry in the world, various innovations are done in order to safeguard our mother earth. The production stages of textile include bleaching, dyeing etc...Contribute to a large extend of pollution thus making it important to make it more sustainable. Controlling pollution is as vital as making a product free from the toxic effect.So in order to safeguard our environment we must take some preventive measures and technologies that can maintain the balance of our eco system and makes the final product free from toxic effects. Generally there is really no such thing as a 100% eco friendly piece of clothing because all clothing takes water (for the fibres to grow) and energy (to make the fabric and the final garments).So, Eco-friendly clothing can be termed as a clothing made of natural fibres such as organic cotton and hemp, clothing that has been organically dyed with vegetables or any fabrics that use small amounts of water, energy and chemicals that affect the environment.

Natural fibres have intrinsic properties such as mechanical strength, low weight and healthier to the wearer that has made them particularly attractive.The word 'eco' is short for ecology. Ecology is the study of the interactions between organisms and their environment. Therefore 'eco' friendly (or 'ecology friendly') is a term to refer to goods and services considered to inflict minimal or no harm on the environment. "Think globally, act locally" is the slogan of tomorrow for the world textile industry.

ECO-FRIENDLY Textiles

Any textile product, which is produced in eco-friendly manner and processed under eco-friendly limits, is known as eco friendly textiles. It is also known as **sustainable fashion**, **eco fashion** and **Ecotech**. Materials can be considered as "Eco-friendly" on the basis of various factors:

- Renewability of the product
- Ecological footprint of resources - how much land it takes for the full growth of a product
- Determining the eco friendliness of a product - amount of chemicals required for the production of products.

TTAIN Eco-Review

We have created our own Fibre Eco-Review, using different resources and studies on the environmental impact of each of the fibres. Here, we have focused on the fibre production.

We have divided fibres in two main categories according to their environmental impact:

- **TTAIN Recomended (TTAIN-R)**
- **TTAIN Not Recommended (TTAIN-NR)**

TTAIN Recomended (TTAIN-R) Fibres

Group A Plant Based	Group B Animal based	Group C Recycled	Group D Semi-Synthetic
Linen	Silk	Recycled Polyester	Pineapple, Corn, Milk, Banana, Orange
Organic Cotton	Alpaca	Recycled Nylon	Lycocell/ Tencel
Hemp	Sustainable Wool	Recycled Cotton	Algae Fibres
Ramie	Sustainable Cashmere	Recycled Wool	Cupro
Natural Rubber	Sustainable Leather	Recycled Textile Fibres	Ayurvastra
Jute	Responsible Down		Soya Bean

TTAIN Not Recomended (TTAIN-NR) Fibres

Group E Natural and Animal Based Fibres		Group F Synthetic and Semi-Synthetic Fibres	
Wool	Leather	Polyester	Acrylic
Cotton	Cashmere	Rayon	Bamboo
Down		Viscose	Vegan Leather
		Modal	Nylon
		Spandex	Polypropylene
		Aramide	PVC

Plant Based

Group A

RECOMMENDED

Group A: Plant Based

Linen

Linen is a natural fibre which stems from the flax plant. It uses considerably fewer resources than cotton or polyester (such as water, energy, pesticides, insecticides, fertilizers).

Flax can grow in poor soil which is not used for food production. In some cases, it can even rehabilitate polluted soil. Flax plants also have a high rate of carbon absorption.

Organic Cotton

The fabric has the same quality as conventional cotton but not the negative impact on the environment. Organic cotton addresses most of the environmental challenges which conventional cotton production faces. It is grown from non-GMO seeds and without the use of pesticide, insecticide or fertilizer. Unlike conventional cotton, organic farmers use ancestral farming methods, including crop-rotation, mixed farming or no-till farming to pre-

serve the soil. Organic cotton uses up to 67% less water than conventional cotton according to some sources. Organic cotton farmers are not exposed to harmful substances. Several organizations have established certifications for organic cotton such as GOTS. Certification is the only proof that a product is truly organic.

Hemp

Hemp fabric comes from the plant with the same name. It is one of the fastest growing plants and it doesn't need much water, energy, pesticide, or fertilizers. The plant is very good for soil, it can be grown for many years in the same place without exhausting it. This is why hemp is considered to be eco-friendly. Hemp has very similar properties to linen. They are often difficult to differentiate. However, as hemp belongs to the same family as cannabis (although it does not have the same psychoactive effects), growing hemp is heavily regulated or prohibited in many countries.

Ramie

Ramie and stinging nettle, or European nettle, are plants used to produced a fibre similar to linen. They are not very common but they are considered sustainable.

Natural Rubber

Synthetic rubber is basically plastic whereas natural rubber is made from the milk of the Hevea tree. Most of the soles of our shoes are nowadays made with synthetic rubber which is a very different thing from natural rubber. Natural rubber, therefore, comes from a renewable resource, the harvesting of rubber doesn't harm trees but actually helps the tree to flourish. It protects forests from being cut down as it gives value to the exploitation of the tree. Rubber is also easy to recycle & biodegradable. Rubber from FSC®-certified forest (IEL, Vol.1, page: 39) is even better as it ensures the good environmental management of the forest.

Jute

Jute fibre is 100% bio-degradable and recyclable and thus environmentally friendly. Jute, an edible leafy vegetable, also known as "the golden fibre", is a long, soft and shiny fibre made from the cellulose and lignin material from the jute plant. A hectare of jute plants consumes about 14.5 tonnes of carbon dioxide and releases 10.5 tonnes of oxygen. Jute also does not generate toxic gases when burnt. Jute reaches maturity quickly, between 5-7 months, making it an incredibly efficient source of renewable material, and therefore "sustainable". Jute products help in decreasing environmental pollution as its use decreases the demand for plastic bags which are non-bio degradable and pollute the surroundings. Jute bags are more useful as compared to the plastic bags as they can be used again and again. **you can simply use jute bags in lieu of non-biodegradable plastic**. Jute is also compostable by itself just like egg shells or the melon peels which means that you can sleep easy knowing that you are not contributing to the pollution or harmful clogging of our environment.

Animal Based

Group B

RECOMMENDED

Group B: Animal Based

Silk

Silk is a protein fibre spun by silkworms and is a renewable resource. Silk is also biodegradable. For these reasons, we consider silk a sustainable fibre. However, chemicals are used to produce conventional silk, so we will always consider organic silk to be a better option. Because conventional silk production kills the silkworm, animal rights advocates prefer "Peace Silk", Tussah, Ahimsa silks which allow the moth to evacuate the cocoon before it is boiled to produce silk.

Alpaca

Alpaca fibre comes from the fleece of the animal bearing the same name. Alpacas are mainly bred in the Peruvian Andes. Alpacas are much more eco-friendly than cashmere goats, because they cut the grass they eat instead of pulling it out, which allows for the grass to keep growing. Additionally, Alpacas have soft padding under their feet, which is more gentle for the soil than goat or sheep hooves.

They need very little water and food to survive and produce enough wool for 4 or 5 sweaters per year while a goat needs 4 years to produce just one cashmere sweater.

Sustainable Wool

Conventional wool is far from being as eco-friendly as we would expect. However, there are some sustainable wool options on the market which make it possible for us to dress warmly and sustainably. So far, we have found the Responsible Wool Standard (RWS), which ensures that farms use best practices to protect the land, and treat the animal decently. Certified organic wool guarantees that pesticides and parasiticides are not used on the pastureland or on the sheep themselves, and that good cultural and management practices of livestock are used. Certified organic wool is still pretty rare on the market. GOTS seems to be the only organization certifying organic wool.

Sustainable Cashmere

As we can see in the related section, conventional cashmere has very significant consequences for the environment.

The good news is that there are a few sustainable cashmere options which address these environmental problems and give us the possibility to buy cashmere without a guilty conscience.

Sustainable Leather

Leather will never be an animal-friendly product: It is made of dead animal skin. However, the skin used to make leather comes from animals raised for their meat. In that sense, it uses a byproduct from another industry, so it doesn't actually need additional land and resources. Conventional leather is heavily criticized for the environmental impact of the tanning process. But leather can also be eco-friendly. There are not many options in the market yet, but they do exist.

Responsible Down

The main issue of conventional down is the live-plucking of birds which is cruel and painful to the animal. For those wanting to use down and enjoy its durability, its lightweight, and warmth, we recommend looking for certified responsible down (Responsible Down Standard) or recycled down.

Recycled

Group C

Group C: Recycled

Recycled polyester

Recycled polyester, often called rPet, is made from recycled plastic bottles. It is a great way to divert plastic from our landfills. The production of recycled polyester requires far fewer resources than that of new fibres and generates fewer CO_2 emissions.

There are 2 ways to recycle polyester: For mechanical recycling, plastic is melted to make new yarn. This process can only be done a few times before the fibre loses its quality. Chemical recycling involves breaking down the plastic molecules and reforming them into yarn. This process maintains the quality of the original fibre and allows the material to be recycled infinitely, but it is more expensive.

Although, Recycled polyester is definitely a sustainable option but, we need to be aware that it is still non-biodegradable and takes years to disappear once thrown away.

Recycled Nylon

Recycled Nylon has the same benefits as recycled polyester: It diverts waste from landfills and its production uses much fewer resources than virgin nylon (including water, energy and fossil fuel).

A large part of the recycled nylon produced comes from old fishing nets. This is a great solution to divert garbage from the ocean. It also comes from nylon carpets, tights, etc. Recycling nylon is still more expensive than new nylon, but it has many environmental advantages. A lot of research is currently being conducted to improve the quality and reduce the costs of the recycling process.

Recycled Cotton

Recycled cotton prevents additional textile waste and requires far fewer resources than conventional or organic cotton. This makes it a great sustainable option. Cotton can be recycled using old garments or textile leftovers. The quality of the cotton may be lower than of new cotton. Recycled cotton is therefore usually blended with new cotton. The production of recycled cotton is still very limited.

Recycled Wool

Recycled wool is also very sustainable option. Apart from diverting used wool garments from landfills, it saves a considerable amount of water, reduces land use for sheep grazing and avoids the use of chemicals for dyeing. Recycled wool contributes to a reduction of air, water, and soil pollution.

Recycled Textile Fibres

A lot of researches are currently going in that direction: making textile from textile waste. As we generate so much textile pre-consumer as well as post-consumer waste, it makes total sense to re-use it instead of throwing it away. However, due to the difficulty to separate fibres blend and other technological challenges, this type of textile is not yet easily available.

Group D

Group D: Semi-Synthetic
Pineapple, Corn, Milk, Bannana and Orange Fibres

Pineapple Fibre (Piñatex)
Piñatex is a fibre that comes from pineapple leaves. It is considered sustainable because it uses the by-products of pineapple harvests, so there is no need for extra resources to produce it. It is used as a substitute for leather.

Corn Fibre
Corn is available in both spun and filament forms. It is derived from naturally occurring plant sugars. It balances strength and resilience with comfort, softness and drape in textiles. Corn also uses no chemical additives or surface treatments and is naturally flame retardant. Corn fibre manufacturers have claimed that these fibres can be used for sportswear, jacket, outer coat, apparels etc.

Milk Fibre
Milk Fibre was firstly introduced in 1930 in Italy & America to compete the wool. It is the new innovative Fibre and a kind of synthetic Fibre made of milk casein Fibre through bio-engineering method. It can also be used to create top-grade underwear, shirts, T-shirts, loungewear, etc. It contains seventeen amino acids & natural anti-bacterial rate is above eighty percent. Hence milk fibre has sanitarian function.

Banana Fibre
The use of banana stems as a source of fibre such as cotton and silk is becoming popular now. It is used all over the world for multiple purposes such as making tea bags or sanitary napkins to Japanese yen notes and car tyres. It is also known as musa fibre which is one of the strongest natural fibres. Banana stem, hitherto considered a complete waste, is now being made into banana-fibre cloth which comes in differing weights and thicknesses based on what part of the banana stem the fibre was taken from. The innermost sheaths are where the softest fibres are obtained, and the thicker and sturdier fibres come from the outer sheaths. High water absorbing property of this fabric makes this clothing cool to wear.

Orange Fibre

Orange Fibre is an innovative fabric made from orange skins that comes from the juice industry wastes.

Lyocell (Tencel)

Lyocell is made in a closed-loop system that recycles almost all of the chemicals used. Lyocell is a manufacturing process of rayon which is much more eco-friendly than its relatives modal and viscose. "Lyocell" is the generic name of the manufacturing process and fibre. Tencel is the brand name of the lyocell commercialized by the company Lenzing AG. Just like rayon and viscose, lyocell is more than 95% biodegradable.

Algae Fibres

Algae are being tapped as a new resource to make fibres, finishes and dyes for the textile industry. Algae bloom can provide cellulose or proteins, and in microalgae form, the species can produce non-petrochemical oils.

The food, pharmaceuticals and biofuels industries have been harnessing the ability of microalgae to produce compounds on an industrial scale for years. Now, a new generation of companies is set on putting this quality to use in developing materials and supplies for textiles, apparel and footwear. Many of the projects involving algae and textiles are still in research phase, but the landscape is changing fast.

Cupro

Cupro is an artificial cellulose fibre made from Linter Cotton (or Cotton wastes). In order to obtain the ready to weave yarn, the extracted cellulose is soaked in a bath of a chemical solution called «cuprammonium », hence the Cupro Name. All the process is made in closed-loop. The large quantities of water and chemicals used in the production of Cupro are therefore constantly reused until they are completely exhausted. The chemicals used are free of toxic or dangerous compounds for health and the environment. Cupro is also biodegradable, so it considers a good eco-friendly alternative to viscose.

Ayurvastra

Ayur vastra is a Sanskrit term made up of two words "AYUR" means "health" & "VASTRA" means "Cloth", meaning "life cloth". It is a branch of Ayurveda. Ayur vastra cloth is completely free from synthetic chemicals & toxic substances making this cloth organic, sustainable & biodegradable. Ayur vastra or medical dress is made of 100% pure organic cotton or silk, wool, jute & coir products that have been hand loomed, dyed by using various Ayurveda herbs & have medicinal qualities. Herb dyed organic fabrics act as healing agents or as an absorber through skin. Each fabric is infused with specific herbs that can help treat skin conditions. Herbs used in Ayur vastra are known to cure allergies having anti-microbial, anti-inflammatory properties Ayur vastra is extra smooth & good for transpiration that helps in recovering various diseases. It may help treat a broad range of diseases such as skin infections, diabetes, eczema, psoriasis, hypertension, high blood pressure, asthma & insomnia.

Soya Bean Fibre

Soybean fibre is a sustainable textile fibre made from renewable natural resources. The soybean protein fibre is actually made from the byproduct leftovers of soybean oil/tofu/soymilk production, which would normally be discarded.

Group E

NOT RECOMMENDED

Cotton

Cotton is mainly produced in dry and warm regions, but it needs a lot of water to grow. In some places, like India, inefficient water use means that more than 19,000 liters of water are needed to produce 1000g of cotton. In the meantime, 100 million people in India do not have access to drinking water. Although it is a natural fibre, conventional cotton is far from environmentally friendly. 97% of cotton is grown using fertilizers and genetically modified seeds. Cotton represents 11% of the pesticides and 27% of the insecticides used globally. 95% of the world's cotton farmers are located in developing countries where labor, health and safety regulations are nonexistent or not enforced most of the time. Child and forced labor are common practice. In some countries, people are forced to pick cotton for little or no pay every year.

Wool

Wool as such is a renewable natural fibre, so it could have been considered an environment-friendly option. Unfortunately, the extensive sheep farming practiced to meet the global demands has had disastrous consequences on the environment. Sheep survive by grazing, which can have a positive impact on certain types of ecosystems when it is well managed. But when the land is grazed too heavily, this leads to overgrazing. Overgrazing means that the vegetation does not have enough time to grow back before it is consumed. The soil becomes weak and vulnerable to erosion and desertification.

For example, 29% of the region of Patagonia is affected by desertification, mainly due to overgrazing by sheep which are primarily raised for their wool. Sheep also release methane, a gas that is 23 times worse for global warming than CO_2. Sheep are often subjected to insecticide baths which contain substances hazardous to the farmers. Residues of those harmful chemicals can remain in the wool and make its way into our clothes. Another concern about wool production is the poor treatment of sheep. When a sheep's fleece is removed (shearing), the shearers often hurt the animals, cutting their skin or hitting them to keep them quiet. Finally, the practice of mulesing has been widely denounced by animal rights activists. Mulesing involves removing the skin of the Merino sheep around the breech to prevent parasitic infection.

Down

Down is the layer of the fine feather of birds. Down has been used for a very long time for insulation and pillows and duvet. It is a light and warm material and very long-lasting. The main sustainability issue with down is that part of the world's supply of down feathers is directly taken ("plucked") on live birds. This practice has been largely denounced due to the suffering of the animal. It is now banned in some countries but still authorized in others. When buying down, it is essential to look for responsible down.

Leather

Leather is a controversial fibre. First of all, it is not an animal-friendly option, since it is made of dead animal skin. But environmental and social concerns related to leather are mostly linked to the tanning process: Toxic chemicals are used (chromium in 79% of cases) to transform the skins into wearable leather. Those substances are often dumped into rivers, polluting freshwater and oceans. Also, most of the tanning factory workers around the world do not wear adequate protection and suffer from skin, eye, and respiratory diseases, cancer and more due to their exposure to chemical substances.

Cashmere

Cashmere fibre comes from cashmere goat hairs. More than 77% of the world's cashmere is produced in China and Mongolia. The main environmental issue stemming from cashmere is due to the fact that goats pull the grass out by the roots when they eat instead of cutting it. As a result, the grass does not grow back, leading to land desertification. This, combined with an overpopulation of goats, results in a real environmental threat.

Mongolia is now suffering the consequences of this overgrazing through cashmere goats. The breeding of more than 21 million cashmere goats is the principal cause of the massive desertification threatening 93% of the surface of the country.

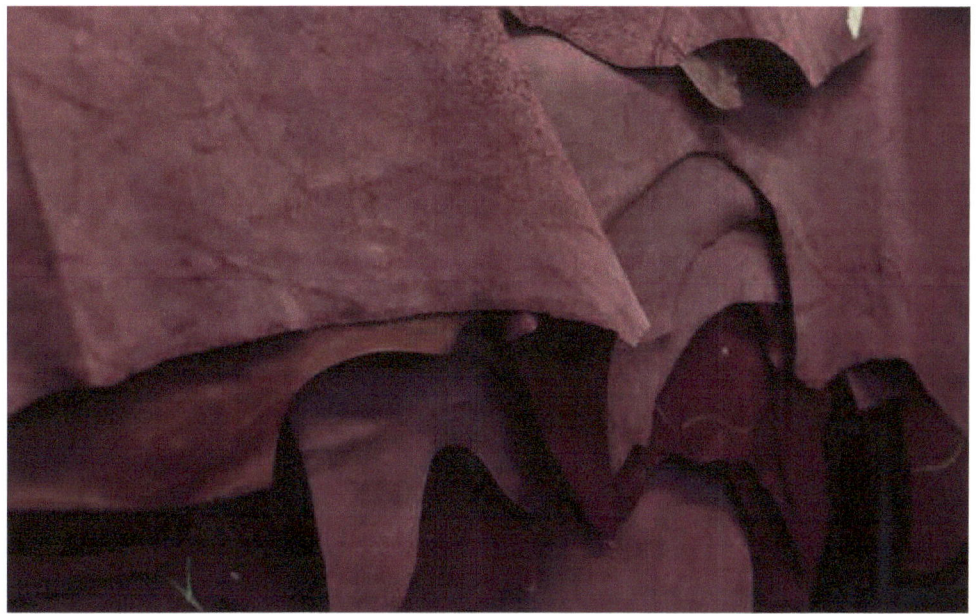

Group F

Not Recommended

Polyester

Polyester is the most common fibre in our garment. We can find it in 55% of our clothes. Polyester is a synthetic fibre derived from petroleum, a non-renewable fossil fuel. As we know, the transformation of crude oil into petrochemicals releases toxins into the atmosphere that are dangerous for human and ecosystem health. The production of polyester also highly energy intensive. One of the major problems with this plastic fibre, is the fact that it is non-biodegradable. Furthermore, each time we wash a polyester garment, it releases 700.000 plastic microfibres, ending up in rivers and oceans and then in our food chain.

Viscose, Rayon, Modal

Viscose (also called Artificial Silk or Art Silk) is the most common type of rayon. Viscose production involves a lot of chemicals, heavily harmful to the environment when they are released in effluents. Rayon is a fibre from regenerated cellulose, generally derived from wood pulp. Rayon is usually made from eucalyptus trees, but any plant can be used (such as bamboo, soy, cotton, etc). To produce the fibre, the plant cellulose goes through a process involving a lot of chemicals, energy and water. Solvents used during the process can be very toxic to humans and to the environment. Viscose, modal, lyocell and bamboo are different types of rayon. The other substantial environmental concerns arising from rayon production is the massive deforestation involved. Thousands of hectares of rainforest are cut down each year to plant trees specifically used to make rayon. Only a very small percentage of this wood is obtained through sustainable forestry practices. Modal, another type of rayon using beech trees with a similar process to viscose. However modal is produced by many other manufacturers who don't necessarily use sustainable processes and it is now rather easy to find sustainable fibres in the market.

Bamboo
Bamboo is usually sold as an eco-friendly textile. Which is partially true, as the bamboo plant is potentially one of the world's most sustainable resource. It grows very quickly and easily, it doesn't need pesticide or fertilizers, and it doesn't need to be replanted after harvest because it grows new sprouts from the roots. However, to turn bamboo into fibre, bamboo is processed with strong chemical solvents that are potentially harmful to the health of manufacturing workers, the consumers wearing the garment, and for the environment when chemicals are released in wastewater.

Acrylic, polyamide, nylon, polypropylene, PVC, spandex
Acrylic, polyamide, nylon, polypropylene, PVC, spandex (AKA lycra or elastane), aramide, etc, are all different types of synthetic fibres that are de-rived from petroleum and therefore have a very similar impact on the envi-ronment as polyester.

Vegan Leather
Vegan leather is usually made of PVC or polyurethane, which are synthetic fibres that have a similar environmental impact to polyester. It is certainly better for animal welfare, but it is not an eco-friendly option. However, some plant-based substitutes of leather exist, such as the pineapple fibre.

Eco-Textiles:
Eco-textiles refers to all fabrics, clothing and accessories that have been manufactured, produced, and processed in an environmentally-conscious manner. This manner reduces any negative impact in the form of pollution or damage to the planet.

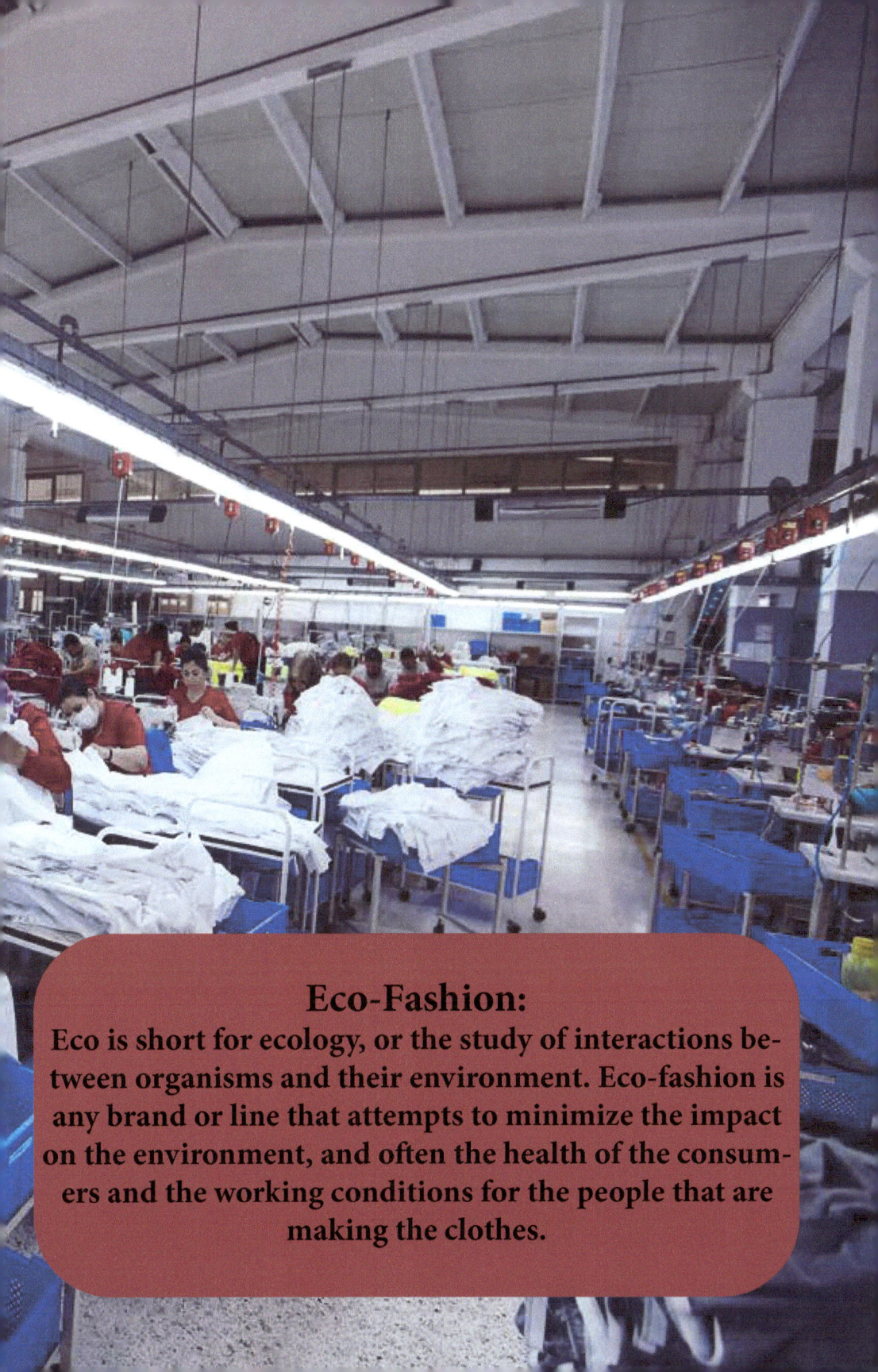

Eco-Fashion:
Eco is short for ecology, or the study of interactions between organisms and their environment. Eco-fashion is any brand or line that attempts to minimize the impact on the environment, and often the health of the consumers and the working conditions for the people that are making the clothes.

CANADA BRONZE BEAVER BADGE

Participate in our Online Classes to earn these exclusive
digital badges!
www.toptenaward.org

Design & Development by:

Tara Asadi

Copyright © 2022 by Top Ten Award International Network.

1) Conventional wool is far from being as _____ as we would expect.
A) economically
B) eco-friendly
C) Chemically
D) Globally
ANSWER:

2) Corn also uses no chemical additives or surface treatments and is naturally flame retardant.
A) True
B) False
ANSWER:

3) Milk Fibre was introduced in 1930 in Italy & America to compete the wool.
A) True
B) False
ANSWER:

4) _____ is a natural fibre which stems from the flax plant.
A) Linen
B) Flannel
C) Jeans
D) Quilted
ANSWER:

5) Cotton is mainly produced in dry and warm regions, but it needs a lot of water to grow. In some places, inefficient water use means that more than 19,000 liters of water are needed to produce 1000g of cotton.
A) True
B) False
ANSWER:

6) In this international manual, we have created our own Fibre Eco-Review using different resources and studies.
A) True
B) False
ANSWER:

7) Determining the eco friendliness of a product - amount of chemicals required.
A) True
B) False
ANSWER:

8) Recycled polyester, often called rpet, is made from recycled plastic bottles.
A) True
B) False
ANSWER:

9) So, it considers a good eco-friendly alternative to viscose. Ayur vastra or medical dress is made of %100 pure organic cotton or silk, wool, jute & coir products that have been hand loomed, dyed by using various Ayurveda herbs & have medicinal qualities.
A) True
B) False
ANSWER:

10) _____ fabric comes from the plant with the same name.
A) Vegetable
B) Wheat
C) Olive
D) Hemp
ANSWER:

11) _____ recycling involves breaking down the plastic molecules and reforming them into yarn.
A) Nano
B) Chemical
C) Physical
D) Deep
ANSWER:

12) _____ have soft padding under their feet, which is more gentle for the soil than goat or sheep hooves.
A) Vegetable
B) Wheat
C) Alpacas
D) Hemp
ANSWER:

13) _____ is a natural fibre which stems from the flax plant.
A) Linen
B) Wheat
C) Olive
D) Hemp
ANSWER:

14) Ramie and stinging nettle, or South American nettle, are plants used to produced.
A) True
B) False
ANSWER:

15) Ramie and stinging nettle, or European nettle, are plants used to produced.
A) True
B) False
ANSWER:

16) Rubber from FSC-certified forest is even better as it ensures the good environmental management of the forest.
A) True
B) False
ANSWER:

17) _____ is an artificial cellulose fibre made from Linter Cotton (or Cotton.
A) Linen   B) Wheat
C) Cupro   D) Hemp
ANSWER:

18) A large part of the recycled nylon produced comes from old fishing nets.
A) True   B) False
ANSWER:

19) _____ from FSC-certified forest is even better as it ensures the good environmental management of the forest.
A) Rubber   B) Cutters
C) Glue   D) Brass
ANSWER:

20) A hectare of jute plants consumes about 14.5 tonnes of carbon dioxide and releases 10.5 tonnes of oxygen.
A) True   B) False
ANSWER:

21) Who is also easy to recycle& biodegradable?
A) Rubber   B) Cutters
C) Glue   D) Brass
ANSWER:

22) The main issue of conventional down is the live-plucking of birds which is cruel and painful to the animal.
A) True   B) False   ANSWER:

23) Algae are being tapped as a new resource to make fibres, finishes and dyes for the textile industry
A) True
B) False
ANSWER:

24) Ayur vastra or medical dress is made of %100 pure organic cotton or silk, wool, jute & coir products that have been hand loomed, dyed by using various Ayurveda herbs & have medicinal qualities.
A) True
B) False
ANSWER:

25) Soybean fibre is a sustainable textile fibre made from renewable natural resources.
A) True
B) False
ANSWER:

26) What is the study of the interactions between organisms and their environment?
A) Geology   B) Biology
C) Ecology   D) Mineralogy
ANSWER:

27) Which of them is Eco-friendly
A) Linen   B) Alpaca
C) Jute   D) All of them
ANSWER:

28) Which of them is Eco-friendly
A) Rayon   B) Nylon
C) Jute   D) Modal
ANSWER:

29) Which of them is NOT Eco-friendly
A) Jute   B) Cupro
C) Ramie   D) Modal
ANSWER:

30) Which of them is NOT Eco-friendly
A) Jute   B) Cupro
C) Ramie   D) Bamboo
ANSWER:

31) Which of them is NOT Eco-friendly
A) Jute   B) Cupro
C) Ramie   D) Leather
ANSWER: D

32) Which of them is NOT Eco-friendly
A) Jute   B) Cupro
C) Ramie   D) PVC
ANSWER:

33) Which of them is Eco-friendly
A) Rayon   B) Nylon
C) Soya Bean   D) Modal
ANSWER:

34) Which of them is Eco-friendly
A) Rayon   B) Nylon
C) Ramie   D) Modal
ANSWER:

35) More than %77 of the world's cashmere is produced in China and
_____.
A) Mongolia   B) Indochina
C) Morocco   D) Ethiopia
ANSWER:

CANADA SILVER BEAVER BADGE

Participate in our Online Classes to earn these exclusive digital badges!
www.toptenaward.org

Design & Development by:

Tara Asadi

Copyright © 2022 by Top Ten Award International Network.

Bibliography:

Andrews, R.N.L. 1998. Environmental regulation and business 'self-regulation'. Policy Sciences 31(3): 177-197.

Apodaca, Julia, "Market Potential of Organically Grown Cotton as a Niche Crop." Natural Fibres Research and Information Center, Bureau of Business Research, University of Texas at Austin, Paper presented at the Beltwide Cotton Conference in Nashville, TN, January 1992.

Asadi, J., "International Environmental Labelling, Economic Consequencies, Export Magazine, July 2001

Asadi, J. 2008. Mobile Phone as management systems tools, ISO Magazine, Vol.8, No.1

Asadi, J., Eco-Labelling Standards, National Standard Magazine, Sep. 2004.

Benitta Christy P & Dr. Kavitha S, "GO-GREEN TEXTILES FOR ENVIRONMENT", Advanced Engineering and Applied Sciences: An International Journal 2014; 4(3): 26-28

Chemical Week, 1999. Europe's Beef Ban Tests Precautionary Principle. (August 11).

CHOI, J.P. Brand Extension as Informational Leverage. Review of Eco- nomic Studies, Vol. 65 (1998), pp. 655-669.

Conway, G. 2000. Genetically modified crops: risks and promise.

Corrado, M., (1989), The Greening Consumer in Britain, MORI, London

Corrado, M., (1997), Green Behaviour – Sustainable Trends, Sustainable Lives?, MORI, london, accessed via countries. Manila, Asian Development Bank 33p.

Deo H T, "Eco friendly textile production", Indian Journal of Fibre & Textile Research Vol.26, March – June 2001,pp.61-73Dawkins, K. 1996. Eco-labeling: consumer's right-to-know or restrictive business practice? Minneapolis, Minn., Institute for Agriculture and Trade Policy.

Di Leva, C. E. 1998. International Environmental Law and Development. Georgetown Interna. Environ. Law Review 10 (2): 502-549.

Economics and Management 43, 339-359.

Eiderstroem, E. 1997. Eco-labeling: Swedish Style. Forum for Applied Research in Public Policy 141(4).

Elkington, J. and Hailes, J. 1990. The green consumer guide: You can buy products that don't cost the earth. New York, Viking Press. 96p.

EMONS, W. Credence Goods and Fraudulent Experts. RAND Journal of Economics, Vol. 28 (1997), pp. 107-119.

EMONS, W. Credence Goods Monopolists. International Journal of In- dustrial Organization, Vol. 19 (2001), pp. 375-389.

Energy.gov, Advantages and Challenges of Wind Energy, Retrieved from: https://www. energy.gov/eere/wind/advantages-and-challenges-wind-energy

Energy.gov, Advantages and Challenges of Wind Energy, Retrieved from: https://www. energy.gov/eere/wind/advantages-and-challenges-wind-energy

Environment Canada 1997. Towards Greener Government Procurement: An Environment Canada Case Study (pp. 31-46). in Greener Purchasing: Opportunities and Innovations.

Environmental Protection Agency 742-R-98-009, (1998),

Environmentalist 17 (2): 125-133.

Erskine, C.C. and Collins, L. 1996. Eco-labeling in the EU: a comparative study of the pulp and paper industry in the UK and Sweden. European Environment 17 (2) : 40-47.

Erskine, C.C. and Collins, L. 1997. "Eco-labeling: Success or failure?".

Ethical Consumer, (1995), Co-op Supermarkets take up Ethics, EC36, June/July, p4

Ethical Consumer, (June 1996), Green Cons, EC41, June, p5

European Communities, Commission of the, 1996. Eco-label revision.

European Communities, Commission of the. 1996. Conservation of West Africa's forests through certification. UN Courier 157: 71-73.

European Union official website: https://ec.europa.eu/info/about-european-commission/ contact_en

Feenstra, R.C. "Exact Hedonic Price Indexes," Review of Economics and Statistics 77 (1995): 634-653.

Feenstra, R.C., and J.A. Levinsohn. "Estimating Markups and Market Conduct with Multidimensional Product Attributes," Review of Economic Studies (62 (1995): 19-52.

Forest Stewardship Council: "Principles and criteria for forest stewardship" Document 1.2: <http://www.fscoax.org>

Forsyth, K. 1999. Will consumers pay more for certified wood products? Journal of Forestry 97 (2) : 18-22.

Freeman, A. M III. The Measurement of Environmental and Resource Values. Theory and Methods. Washington D.C.: Resource for the Future, 1993.

Friends of the Earth, 1993. Timber certification and eco-labeling. London, FOE:

Geetha Margret Soundri, "Ecofriendly Antimicrobial Finishing of Textiles Using Natural Extract", Journal of International Academic Research For Multidisciplinary, ISSN: 2320 − 5083, 2014, Vol 2.

Graves, P., J.C. Murdoch, M.A. Thayer, and D. Waldman. "The Robustness of Hedonic Price Estimation: Urban Air Quality," Land Economics 64(1988): 220-233.

Halvorsen, R. and R. Palmquist. "The Interpretation of Dummy Variables in Semiloga-rithmic Equations." American Economic Review 70:474-75 (1980).

Imhoff, Dan, and Grose, Lynda, and Carra, Roberto., "Organic Cotton Exhibit," Mimeo. Simple Life and distributed the Texas Organic Cotton Marketing Cooperative, O'Don-nell, Texas (1996).

Imhoff, Dan. "Growing Pains: Organic Cotton Tests the Fibre of Growers and Manufac-turers Alike," reprinted on Simple Life's web page (simplelife.com), but first printed by Farmer to Farmer, December 1995.

Incomplete Consumer Information in Laboratory Markets. Journal of Environmental labeling.

ISO 14020, ISO 14021,ISO 14024,ISO 14025, International Organization for Standardization.

Kennedy, P.E. "Estimation with Correctly Interpreted Dummy Variables in Semilogarith-mic Equations," American Economic Review 71: 801 (1981).

Kirchho®, S., (2000), Green Business and Blue Angels.

Kraus, Jeff. Lab Technician at the North Carolina School of Textiles.

Labeling Issues, Policies and Practices Worldwide.

Lamport, L. 1998. The cast of (timber) certifiers: who are they? International J. Ecofor-estry 11(4): 118-122.

Large Scale impoverishment of Amazonian forests by logging and fire. 1999.

Lathrop, K.W. and Centner, T.J. 1998. Eco-labeling and ISO 14000: An analysis of US regulatory systems and issues concerning adoption of type II standards. Environmental

Lee, J. et al. 1996. Trade related environmental measures; sizing and comparing impacts.

Lehtonen, Markku. 1997. Criteria in Environmental Labeling: A comparative Analysis on Environmental Criteria in Selected Labeling Schemes. Geneva, UNEP. 148p.

LIEBI, T. Trusting Labels: A Matter of Numbers? Working Paper Uni versity of Bern, No. 0201 (2002).

Lindstrom, T. 1999. Forest Certification: The View from Europe's NIPFs. Journal of Forestry 97(3): 25-31. London

Losey, J.E., Rayor, L.S. & Carter, M.E. 1999. Transgenic pollen harms monarch larvae. Nature 399 20 May): p.214.

Management 22 (2) : 163-172.

Mattoo, A. and H. V. Singh, (1994), Eco-Labelling: Policy Considera-Michaels, R. G., and V. K. Smith. "Market Segmentation And Valuing Amenities With Hedonic Models: The Case Of Hazardous Waste Sites," Journal of Urban Economics, 1990 28(2), 223-242.

Mintel, (1991), The Green Consumer I, May

Mintel, (1994), The Green Consumer, Mintel Special Report

Moraga-Gonzalez, J. L. and N. Padr¶on-Fumero, (2002),

NCC, (1996a), Green Claims – a consumer investigation into marketing claims about the environment,

NCC, (1996b), Shades of Green – consumers' attitudes to green shopping, National Consumer Council,

Nelson , P."Information and Consumer Behaviour," Journal of Political Economy 78 (1970): 311-329..

Nicholson-Lord, D., (1993) 'Tis the Season to be Green, The Independent, 20 December

Nuttall, N., (1993), Shoppers can cross green products off their lists, The Times, 3 July

OCDE/GD(97)105. Paris, OECD. 81p.

OECD. "Ec-labelling: Actual Effects of Selected Programmes," OCDE/GD (97) 105, 1997, Paris. (available on line at http://www.oecd.org/env/eco/books.htm#trademono)

OECD. 1997a. Case study on eco-labeling schemes. Paris, OECD (30 Dec):

OECD. 1997b. Eco-labeling: Actual Effects of Selected Programs.

Osborne, L. "Market Structure, Hedonic Models, and the Valuation of Environmental Amenities." Unpublished Ph.D. dissertation. North Carolina State University, 1995.

Osborne, L., and V. K. Smith. "Environmental Amenities, Product Differentiation, and market Power," Mimeo, 1997.

Ozanne, L.K. and Vlosky, R.P. 1996. Wood products environmental certification: the United States perspective". Forestry Chronicle 72 (2) : 157-165.

Palmquist, R. B., F. M. Roka, and T.Vukina. "Hog Operations, Environmental Effects, and Residential Property Values," Land Economics 73(1), (1997): 114-24.

Palmquist, R.B. "Hedonic Methods," in J.B Braden and C.D. Kolstad, eds. Measuring the Demand for Environmental Improvement. Amsterdam, NL: Elsevier, 1991.

Pento, T. 1997. Implementation of Public Green Procurement Programs (22-31) in Greener Purchasing: Opportunities and Innovations. Sheffield, Greenleaf Publ. 325 p.

Perloff, J. "Industrial Organization Lecture Notes," Mimeo. University of California at Berkeley (1985).

Plant, C. and Plant, J. 1991. Green business: hope or hoax? Philadelphia, New Society Publishers 136 p.

Polak, J. and Bergholm, K. 1997. Eco-labeling and trade: a cooperative approach (Jan.): Policy in a Green Market. Environmental and Resource Economics 22, 419-

Poore, M.E.D. et al. 1989. No timber without trees. London, Earthscan. 352p.

Raff, D. M.G., and M. Trajtenberg. "Quality-Adjusted Prices for the American Automobile Industry: 1906-1940." NBER Working Paper Series, Working Paper No. 5035, February 1995.

Rastogi, J. 1998. What's Behind the Label? Complexities of Certified Wood. Ecoforestry 13 (2): 38-42.

Rinsey Antony V A, "Green and Safe Textiles", Solutions to Ecological Challenges: Multidimensional Perspectives, ISBN No: 978-81-926370-2-0, Pg 291-294, Reflection Books

Roberts, J. T. 1998. Emerging global environment standards: prospects and perils. Journal of Developing Societies 14 (1): 144-163.

Rosen, S., "Hedonic Prices and Implicit Markets: Product Differentiation in Pure Competition." Journal of Political Economy. 82: 34-55 (1974).

Ross, B. 1997. Eco-friendly procurement training course for UN HCR. : 126 p.

Ryan, S., and Skipworth, M., (1993), Consumers turn their backs on green revolution, The Times, 4 April

Salzman, J. 1997. Informing the Green Consumer: The Debate over the Use and Abuse of Environmental Labels. Journal of Industrial Ecology 1 (2): 11-22.

Sanders, W. 1997. Environmentally Preferable Purchasing: The US Experience (946-960) in Greener Purchasing: Opportunities and Innovations. Sheffield, Greenleaf Publ. 325p.

Sayre, D. 1996. Inside ISO 14000: The competitive advantage of environmental management. Delray Beach FL., St. Lucie Press. 232p.

SHAPIRO, C. Premiums for High Quality Products as Returns to Reputa- tion. Quarterly Journal of Economics, Vol. 98, No. 4 (1983), pp. 659-680.

Stillwell, M. and van Dyke, B. 1999. An activists handbook on genetically modified organisms and the WTO. Washington DC., The Consumer's Choice Council: 20 p.

Teisl, M. F., B. Roe, and R. L. Hicks. "Can Eco-labels tune a market? Evidence from dolphin-safe labeling," Presented paper at the 1997 American Agricultural Economics Association Meetings, Toronto.

THE GERSEN, C. Psychological Determinants of Paying Attention to Eco- Labels in Purchase Decisions: Model Development and Multinational Vali- dation. Journal of Consumer Policy, Vol. 23, No. 4 (2000), pp. 285-313.

Tibor, T. and Feldman, I. 1995. ISO 14000: a guide to the new environmental management standards. Burr Ridge Ill., Irwin Professional Publ. 250 p.

Torre, I. de la, & Batker, D. K. (n.d.) 1999-2000. Prawn to trade: prawn to consume. Graham WA., Industrial Shrimp Action Network (isatorre@seanet.com), [and] Asia –Pacific

Townsend, M. 1998. Making things greener: motivations and influences in the greening of manufacturing. Aldershot, England, Ashgate Publisher. 203p.

U.S. Energy Information Administration, What is U.S. Electricity Generation by Energy Source?, Retrieved From: https://www.eia.gov/tools/faqs/faq.php?id=427&t=3

U.S. Energy Information Administration, Biomass Explained, Retrieved From: https://www.eia.gov/energyexplained/?page=biomass_home

U.S. Environmental Protection Agency. National Water Quality Fact Inventory: 1990 Report to Congress. EPA 503-9-92-006, Apr. 1992.

UK Eco-labelling Board website, accessed via http://www.ecosite.co.uk/Ecolabel-UK/

US Environmental Protection Agency (EPA742-R-99-001): 40 p. <www.epa.gov/opptintr/epp>

US EPA, 1993. Determinants of effectiveness for environmental certification and labeling programs. Washington, D.C., US Environmental Protect

US EPA, 1993. Status report on the use of environmental labels worldwide. Washington, D.C., US Environmental Protection Agency (742-R-93-001 September).

US EPA, 1993. The use of life-cycle assessment in environmental labeling. Washington, D.C., US Environmental Protection Agency (742-R-93-003 September).

US EPA, 1998. Environmental labeling: issues, policies, and practices worldwide. Washington DC., Environmental Protection Agency, Pollution Prevention Division Prepared by Abt

US EPA, 1999. Comprehensive procurement guidelines (CPG) program. Washington, D.C., US Environmental Protection Agency: <www.epa.gov/cpg>

US EPA, 1999. Environmentally preferable purchasing program: Private sector pioneers: How companies are incorporating environmentally preferable purchases. Washington, D.C.,

USG, 1993. Federal acquisition, recycling, and waste prevention. Washington DC., Executive Order: (20 October).

USG, 1998. Greening the government through waste prevention, recycling, and federal acquisition. Washington, D.C., Executive Order 13101 (September).

Van der Grijp, N. 1998. The Greening of Public Procurement in the Netherlands (60-71) in Greener Purchasing: Opportunities and Innovations. Sheffield, Greenleaf Pub. 325 p.

Vanclay, J.K. 1996. Lessons from the Queensland rainforests: steps towards sustainability. J. Sustainable Forestry 3 (2/3): 1-25.

Vidal, J., (1993), Shopping for a paler shade of green, The Guardian, 7 April

Voluntary Overcompliance. Journal of Economic Behavior and Organization

Von Felbert, D. 1995. Trade, environment and aid. Paris, OECD Observer 195: 6-10.

Ward, H. 1997. Review of European Community and International Environmental Law 6 (2): 139-147.

Wasik, John, F. Green Marketing and Management: a Global Perspective, Blackwell Business: Cambridge, Mass, 1996.

West, K. 1995. Ecolabels: the industrialization of environmental standards. The Ecologist (Jan/Feb) 25: 16-20.

Worcester, R., (1995), Business and the Environment – in the aftermath of Brent Spar and BSE, MORI,

World Commission on Forests and Sustainable Development: Final Report. <http://iisd. ca/wcfsd>.

Zarrilli, S., V. Jha, and R. Vossenaar, eds. Eco-labelling and International Trade, St martin Press, Inc. New-York, 1997.

Environmental Lifestyle Guide

For Grade 9

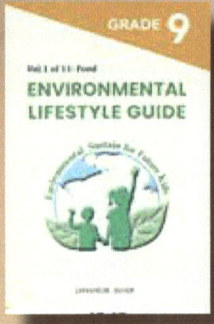 

For Grade 10

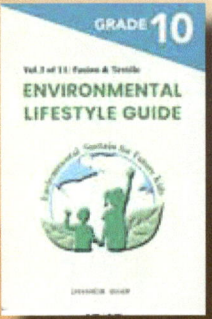  

Plus Online Certification Tests via:
https://toptenaward.org

Standard Text Books

For Grade 11

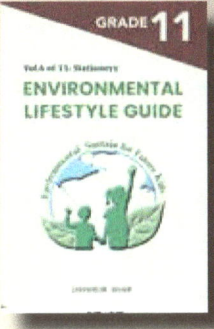

For Grade 12

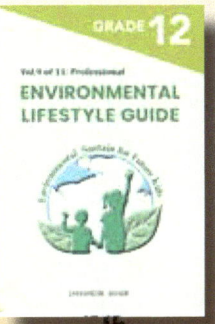
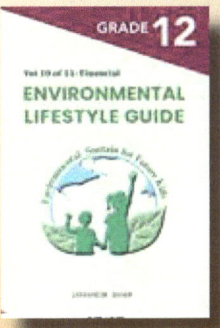

**Environmental Lifestyle Guide
Standard Text Book**
For Students Grade 9 to 12
Available in more than
39,000 Bookstores
all over the globe.
https://ecofriendlyeducation.com

Cooperation by:
Top Ten Award International Network
&
Environmental Sustain for Future Kids

www.ingramcontent.com/pod-product-compliance
Lightning Source LLC
Chambersburg PA
CBHW040858120626
46551CB00001B/69